Let's Explore
MINI BEASTS

Illustrated by Barry Green and Repro India Ltd

TOP THAT! Kids™

Published by Top That! Publishing plc
Tide Mill Way, Woodbridge, Suffolk, IP12 1AP, UK
www.topthatpublishing.com
Top That! Kids is a Trademark of Top That! Publishing plc

Exploring Mini Beasts

The world is just heaving with small creatures, buzzing, burrowing, scuttling, creeping and lurking all around us!

There are masses of micro monsters everywhere!

- In pools and rivers
- In fields and parks
- In oceans
- In homes and gardens
- On plants and flowers
- In woodland and rainforests
- In soil

Safe Hunting

Remember to always ask an adult to accompany you on your expeditions, especially if you're visiting ponds or rivers!

There's no escape! They're even on our bodies and in our beds, like this horrible-looking bedbug pictured below.

A microscopic view of the horrible bedbug!

Getting Started

You must handle bugs kindly, without causing them harm.

Being a successful bug-hunter involves patience and cunning. You can use the bug catcher, net and jars in the pack to capture bugs to study.

Try one of these methods to catch bugs without causing them pain and panic.

1. Bury a jar in the ground. This is called a pitfall, and it collects night-crawlers while you are comfortably tucked up in bed.

2. Spread an old sheet on the ground, then bang on a branch with a stick. The bugs will rain down, so be sure you wear a hat!

Nasty Bugs

It makes sense not to touch any bug unless you are really sure that what you catch won't hurt you.

Remember: Always release bugs after you have finished looking at them.

Pooter Jar

A Pooter jar will help you to snap up the tiniest creatures as fast as a bird!

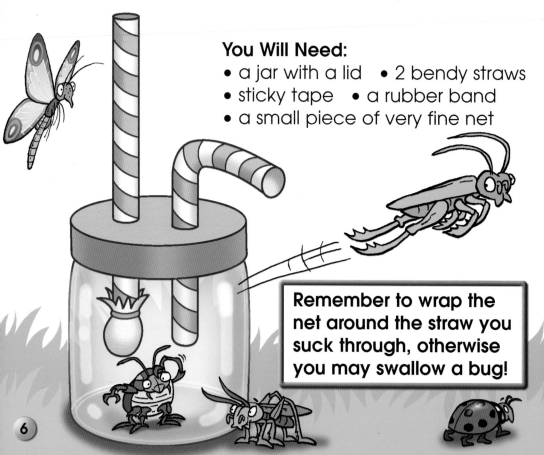

You Will Need:
- a jar with a lid
- 2 bendy straws
- sticky tape
- a rubber band
- a small piece of very fine net

Remember to wrap the net around the straw you suck through, otherwise you may swallow a bug!

1. First remove the lid from the jar then ask an adult to make two holes in it.

2. Now push one straw through each hole. If the holes are too big, stick some tape around them to hold the straws in place.

3. Push one straw in deeper than the other – this will be the straw that the bug shoots down!

4. Wrap the fine net around the end of the other straw and secure with the elastic band.

5. Put the lid back onto the jar and it's ready!

Using the Pooter is very simple. Spot a bug, then suck on the straw with net on the end. The bug should shoot through the other straw into the jar and land unhurt!

Beastly Bodies

Here's a guide to some of the groups that form part of the creepy-crawly world.

Arthropods

Arthropods are a group of creatures that have certain things in common:
- they have no backbone.
- they have a skeleton outside of their bodies.

There are more than one million arthropods, including:
- insects
- arachnids
- crustaceans
- myriapods

A Colorado beetle

Insects

Insects, such as bees, have six legs and three body parts – a head, thorax and abdomen.

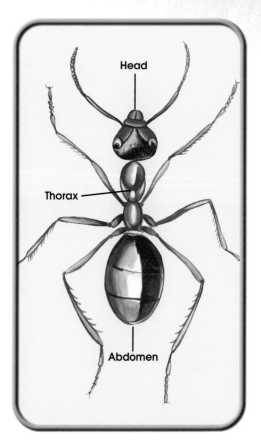

Head

Thorax

Abdomen

Arachnids

Arachnids, like spiders, have eight legs.

Crustaceans

These are arthropods that live in the sea! Members of this family include lobsters and crabs.

Myriapods

A myriapod is a creature that has a long body and many legs – like centipedes!

Spiders

The word 'spider' is enough to make many people jump!

A black widow spider

Crush Prey

All spiders are meat-eaters. Most spiders inject fluid into a victim to dissolve the contents of their body, allowing them to then suck out the remains!

Sticky Webs

Not all spiders weave webs to catch their prey, but many of them make silk inside their body and use it to spin sticky webs to catch creatures such as flies and wasps.

The web is sticky to trap prey.

Tarantulas

Tarantulas, also known as bird eating spiders, are fast runners. They come out to hunt their prey, which includes mice, at night.

A tarantula

Poison

The most poisonous spider in the world is the Brazilian hunting spider whose bite can kill a person in hours!

Flies

Not all insects that fly are flies!

Compound eyes - cover most of the head's surface

Mouthparts - designed for sucking

Thorax - contains muscles to move front wings

Antennae - flies use these to examine food

Bristly abdomen

A housefly

Veiny wings

Habitats

Flies live all over the world – in tropical rainforests, in water, at the Arctic – where they suck the juice from plants or other creatures.

Viruses and Bacteria

House flies can spread very serious diseases and bacteria (germs). They can also be a nuisance by destroying plants.

Mosquitoes

Mosquitoes are a nuisance because they spread horrible diseases. They prefer warm countries and like living in woodland areas near to water.

Ants

Ants are related to wasps, and are also very serious about protecting their nests.

Ant Colony

Every ant has a special role to play in a colony. There are queens for laying eggs (usually a single queen for a colony), males for making babies (larvae) with the queen, and workers, who look after the babies, feed the colony and tend the nest.

A colony of fire ants.

Leafcutter Ants

Leafcutter ants come from
Central and South America. They eat a
diet of fungus that they grow themselves. Leaves are
carried deep underground, licked clean, cut up into
a gooey mulch, and pooed on!

Leafcutter ants

Army Ants

Army ants are very aggressive,
raiding other ant colonies and
even capturing slaves!

Swarms

Travelling in swarms (big
groups), ants nibble on
everything in their path – and
that really does mean anything,
including sleepy buffaloes.

A swarm of ants on the move

Beetles

There are around 30,000 species of beetle, much more than any other insect!

Beetles can be found in many beautiful colours.

Wing Power

You can easily recognise a beetle by looking at its wings. The front wings are very tough. They are not used to fly with, but help to protect the back wings, which fold underneath when the beetle rests.

Lovely Ladybird

You've probably heard of a few beetles before, but did you know the ladybird is also a beetle?

Two ladybirds

Yuck

Dung beetles love poo! Without these useful little creatures, there would be masses of yucky piles of muck all over the place, just waiting for us to tread in!

Hungry Beetle

A single dung beetle can eat its own weight in dung in 24 hours. Over the course of a year, it can bury around half a tonne of the stuff.

A dung beetle

Bees

Like ants, bees are social insects. They live together in colonies.

Nectar Collection

Honeybees collect nectar from flowers and store it in a special sac. They take the nectar back to the hive where they spread it on the roof and fan it with their wings to remove moisture. Then a layer of wax is added – this is how honey is made.

A bumblebee

Bees in a hive

Killer Bees

Killer bees were created by scientists who were attempting to make a 'super' honeybee that could produce more honey. The killer bees were accidentally released into South and North America and are now a big threat to normal honeybees.

A bee sting

Deadly Swarm

These bees are very aggressive, and a swarm of them can be deadly to humans! Even if you dive underwater to avoid them, they'll wait around until you surface!

Killer bees

Butterflies and Moths

Butterflies can only be seen during the daytime but moths usually come out at night.

Life cycle of a Butterfly

Once a butterfly has laid its eggs, it no longer stays with them. Caterpillars hatch from these eggs and begin eating – a lot! Later, caterpillars form chrysalises in which they spend about two weeks resting. An amazing transformation takes place during this time and the caterpillar emerges from its chrysalis as a butterfly!

Little and Large

Atlas moths are the largest moths in the world, with a wingspan of up to 25 cm, while pygmy moths, with a wingspan of 5 mm, are the smallest.

An Atlas moth

Brazilian Moth

Found in southern Brazil, the Brazilian moth will extend its brightly-coloured abdomen to scare off predators.

Munching Lunch

If you find some tiny holes in your woolly jumper, it could have been eaten. Although it is commonly believed that moths eat clothes it is, in fact, just the moth larvae.

A Brazilian moth

Wasps

Most of us would easily recognise a wasp because of its black and yellow stripes.

Queen and Workers

Like ants and honeybees, social wasps live in colonies, with a queen and lots of workers. The workers feed chewed-up insects to the growing larvae. Wasps live all over the world and measure around 10-35 mm long.

A wasps' nest

Some wasps lay eggs inside other insects. The larvae feed on the victim's body before chewing their way out.

Wasp larvae eating their way out of the victim's body.

Hornets

Hornets are a large species of social wasp, measuring 22–30 mm long – the biggest stinging insect in the world! They nest in hollow trees, in riverbanks or underneath roofs.

Digger Wasps

Digger wasps are also know as 'hunting wasps', measuring up to 5 cm long. They live all over the world, and nest in rotted wood, plant stems or soil.

A digger wasp

Bugs and Earwigs

The word 'bug' is used by many of us to describe any old creepy crawly but, in fact, bugs are a special type of insect!

Assassin Bugs and Ambush Bugs

Both assassin bugs and ambush bugs use their mouth to suck out the contents of a victim's body! Assassin bugs live mainly in tropical areas in the Americas and Asia. They lie in wait on plants or flowers for insects to go past, then lunge at them with their front legs.

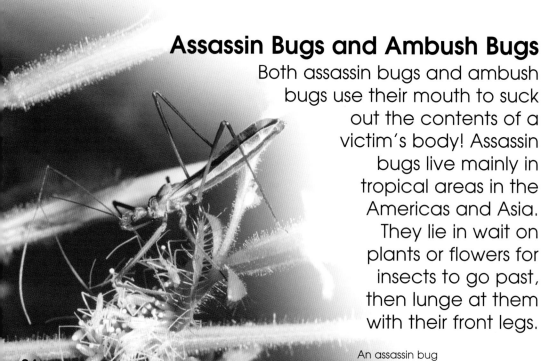

An assassin bug

Body Fluids

While the victim is held tight, the assassin bug inserts its short beak and slurps up the body fluids!

Kissing Bugs

Kissing bugs are a type of ambush bug. They get their name from their habit of biting people around the mouth at night. They are nasty nippers that can spread disease.

A kissing bug

Sick!

Female earwigs look after their young until they can care for themselves, which is very unusual for insects. They feed their nymphs on meals of sicked-up food!

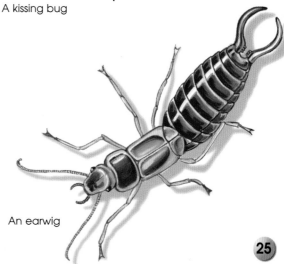

An earwig

25

Grasshoppers and Crickets

The name 'grasshopper' is often used to describe both grasshoppers and crickets.

Two Groups

There are two main groups of grasshoppers, long-horned and short-horned (horn is another word for antenna); the short-horned grasshoppers are what we call locusts. Crickets are also related to grasshoppers and locusts.

A Locust

A house cricket

Snow Crickets

These are also called thermometer crickets, because it is believed that if you count the number of chirps they make in 15 seconds and add on 40, this should give you the temperature in Fahrenheit.

Different Habitats

Grasshoppers and crickets particularly like warm grasslands, where they eat plants, leaves and grass, chewing them up with their tough mouthparts.

Special Jump

These creatures can leap so well because of their long, strong back legs. A grasshopper can leap 20 times the length of its own body!

Millipedes and Centipedes

You'll be lucky if you ever see
one of these many-legged monsters,
as they like to live in moist, dark places.

Millipedes

Millipedes

The name 'millipede' means
'one thousand legs', but no
millipede has more than 750.
Perhaps because they have
so many legs to control,
millipedes are slow
movers, crawling
through soil
and leaves.

Protection

As they are slow, millipedes cannot easily run away from danger. Instead, some species use bright colours or release chemicals to warn off predators.

Centipedes

Centipedes are faster movers than millipedes, and more aggressive. They are predators, hunting insects for food, which they kill will their poisonous claws.

Habitat

Like millipedes, centipedes live in leaf litter and soil, under stones and rotting wood, although some species live in buildings.

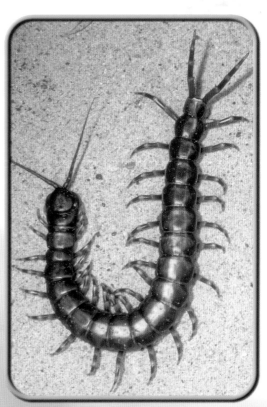

A centipede

Dragonflies and Damselflies

Dragonflies and damselflies have been around for many millions of years!

An emperor dragonfly

Brightly Coloured Beauties

Dragonflies and damselflies look similar, with long, slender, often brightly coloured bodies and see-through wings. When young they live as nymphs in water, only leaving it as adults.

Bulging Eyes

A dragonfly has huge, bulging eyes that cover most of its head, allowing it to see all around. Damselflies' eyes are spaced far apart.

Dragonflies have big, bulging eyes.

Similar Wings

You can tell a dragonfly apart from a damselfly if you compare their wings. When resting, damselflies hold their wings together, bug dragonflies hold their wings out to the side.

A damselfly

Excellent Predators

Dragonflies and damselflies are both excellent hunters in the air, snapping up flying insects.

Worms

Worms do not belong to the same big group as the rest of the 'micro monsters' in this book.

Flat Flukes

Flukes are otherwise known as flatworms, because their body is flat like a ribbon. Flukes live inside the bodies of animals such as fish, dogs and humans, and they cause disease.

A fluke

Tapeworms

Tapeworms are also known as flatworms. Like flukes, they live in the bodies of animals. The use hooks and suckers to attach themselves to their host.

A Gardener's Best Friend

Earthworms tunnel underground, letting air in as they plough the soil. They eat rotting plants and turn them into brilliant fertiliser where it is needed.

An earthworm

Nematodes

Nematodes are also known as roundworms. They live in soil, mud and sand – even in snow. There can be thousands of them in just one square metre of earth!

Spiders – Spot It

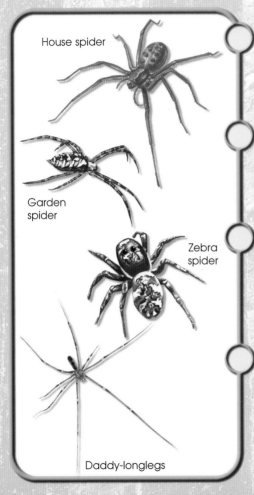

House spider

Garden spider

Zebra spider

Daddy-longlegs

House Spider
These spiders have a large, globe-shaped abdomen with several dark stripes.

Garden Spider
Look for it in the garden where it will be busy spinning a circular web.

Zebra Spider
The zebra spider quietly stalks its prey until it gets close enough to attack and paralyse it with its jaws.

Daddy-longlegs
This spider has long, skinny legs which come in very handy for catching prey.

Flies – Spot It

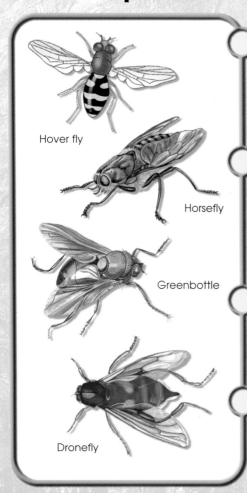

Hover fly

Horsefly

Greenbottle

Dronefly

Hover Fly
These are one of the few insects that can fly backwards. Spot it on hogweed during the summer.

Horsefly
Have you ever seen cows flicking their tails in the hot sun? Look a little closer and you'll probably spot the horsefly buzzing around.

Greenbottle
The greenbottle is metallic green in colour. It lays its eggs on egg, fish and meat.

Drone Fly
The drone fly gets its name from its similarity to a male honeybee. You can spot it in the spring.

Bees – Spot It

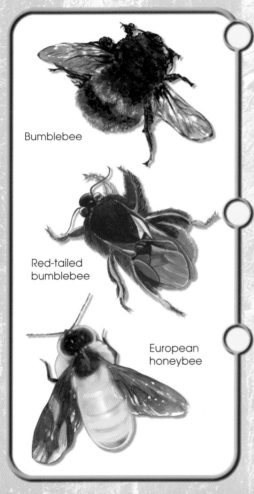

Bumblebee

Red-tailed
bumblebee

European
honeybee

Bumblebee
Bumblebees can be seen buzzing around a summer garden, pollinating flowers. They are round and furry, live in small nests and are not aggressive.

Red-tailed Bumblebee
This bee has bright red hairs at the tip of its abdomen and is about 23 mm long.

European Honeybee
You can spot the males in summer. Most honeybees live in artificial hives where they are looked after by humans for their honey.

Ants – Spot It

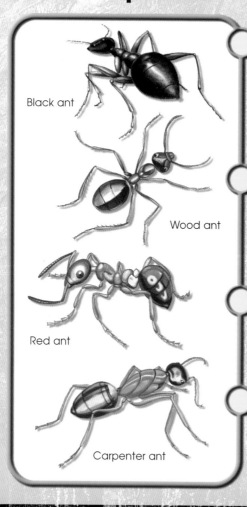

Black ant

Wood ant

Red ant

Carpenter ant

Black Ant
Sometimes called the black garden ant, you can easily spot this ant nesting underneath the garden path or under stones outside.

Wood Ant
Wood ants are 5–10 mm long and build nests from large mounds of leaves and twigs in wooded areas.

Red Ant
Red ants are 5–10 mm long and are common visitors to the garden.

Carpenter Ant
These large ants are 6–19 mm long and are either black, or black/red in colour. They nest in fallen trees and timber.

Beetles – Spot It

Glow-worm

Stag beetle

Vine weevil

Glow-worm
The male glow-worm is 10–13 mm long; the female has pale yellow patches underneath her abdomen which give out a greenish light.

Stag Beetle
The mighty stag beetle is one of the largest beetles in Europe, at around 28 mm long.

Vine Weevil
Vine weevils are vegetarian, feeding on a diet of seeds and plants. They are very unpopular with gardeners and farmers as they can do a lot of damage to gardens and crops.

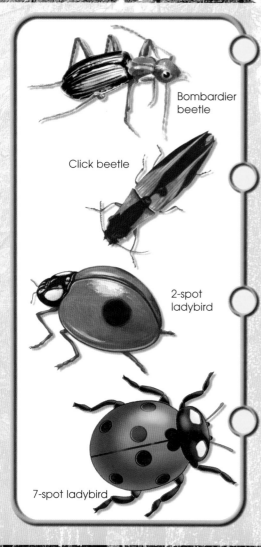

Bombardier beetle

Click beetle

2-spot ladybird

7-spot ladybird

Bombardier Beetle

If you spot this beetle, watch out! It has the amazing ability to spray jets of boiling hot, toxic chemicals from its rear end.

Click Beetle

If it finds itself upside-down, this beetle leaps into the air to right itself, making a loud 'click' as it does so!

2-spot Ladybird

The 2-spot ladybird is 4–5 mm long and is a common sight in the summer. They vary in colour - some are black with red spots!

7-spot Ladybird

This is one of the easiest ladybirds to spot and also one of the biggest. Look for it in the garden, where it feasts on aphids.

Bugs and Water Beetles – Spot It

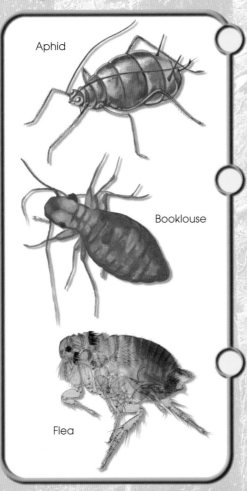

Aphid

Booklouse

Flea

Aphid

Aphids like to suck sap from plants, making the plants weak. You can easily spot them on roses in the spring.

Booklouse

The booklouse lives in houses, scavenging on plant and animal matter. It can be spotted chewing the glue of bookbindings, wallpaper and even stamps!

Flea

The most common household flea is the cat flea. It is easy to spot on pale fur because the dried blood from its bites give the appearance of dirt.

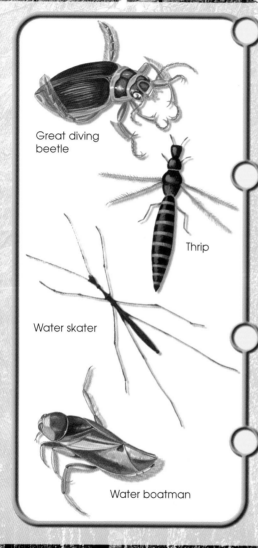

Great diving beetle

Thrip

Water skater

Water boatman

Great Diving Beetle

This impressive water beetle is 60 mm long. Look for it in ponds and lakes where it is a fierce predator, even attacking frogs and fish!

Thrip

Thrips are commonly known as thunder flies because they often appear in stormy weather. They are tiny, black or brown with yellow bands and have four feathery wings.

Water Skater

These creatures group together in large numbers, moving over the surface of quiet ponds.

Water Boatman

The water boatman can be as long as 15 mm. Look for it lurking in the vegetation of still and fast-flowing ponds.

Millipedes and Centipedes – Spot It

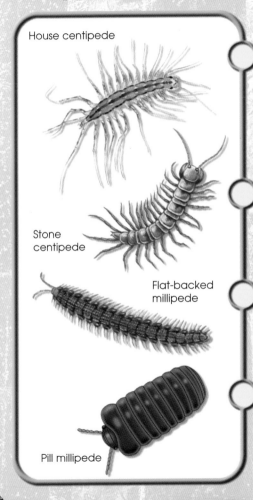

House centipede

Stone centipede

Flat-backed millipede

Pill millipede

House Centipede
All centipedes are predators and have poisonous fangs curving around their head. They like to hide in the day, coming out to hunt at night.

Stone Centipede
This centipede should be an easy spot, as it lurks under logs and stones almost anywhere.

Flat-backed Millipede
It lives in leaf litter so you are most likely to spot it in a compost heap.

Pill Millipede
Millipedes usually come out at night when there is less risk of being eaten by toads and starlings.

Wasps – Spot It

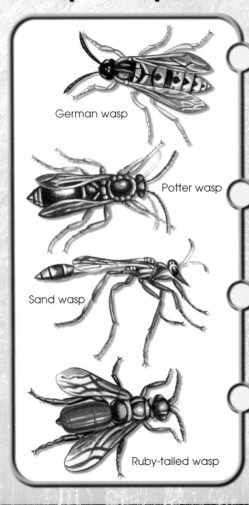

German wasp

Potter wasp

Sand wasp

Ruby-tailed wasp

German Wasp
The German wasp is about 18 mm long, with typical wasp colourings and markings. See if you can find it in your garden.

Potter Wasp
The potter wasp is black and white, with yellow or red markings and is 9–20 mm long.

Sand Wasp
Sand wasps are so called because they make their nests in sandy ground.

Ruby-tailed Wasp
This wasp is small with a green shiny head and thorax, and ruby coloured abdomen.

Butterflies and Moths – Spot It

Purple hairstreak

Red admiral

Cabbage white

Purple Hairstreak Butterfly
Both the male and female have bold purple markings on the upper side of their wings, but only the male is lilac underneath. Purple hairstreaks tend to fly high in oak forests.

Red Admiral Butterfly
This beautiful butterfly is easily recognised by its bold red stripes, orange-tipped underside and white spots.

Cabbage White Butterfly
This medium-sized, relatively common butterfly is often spotted in gardens. Unlike other 'white' butterflies, which have extensive black markings, this species is virtually green-white all over.

Peacock

Vapourer

Hummingbird moth

Elephant hawk moth

Peacock Butterfly

The brightly coloured butterfly is decorated with unusual 'eye' markings – used to scare away predators, like birds.

Vapourer Moth

The female vapourer moth is wingless, while the male is stout and hairy. The female likes to stay in her cocoon, but the male ventures outside.

Hummingbird Moth

The hummingbird moth has brown forewings, orange hindwings and a white-banded abdomen.

Elephant Hawk Moth

This moth has a wingspan of 45–60 mm, distinctive pink colouring and hairy antennae. All hawk moths are powerful fliers (hence their name).

Earwigs and Cockroaches – Spot It

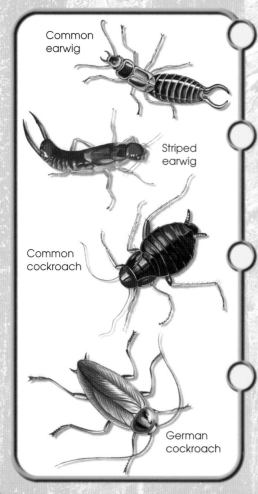

Common earwig

Striped earwig

Common cockroach

German cockroach

Common Earwig
The common earwig eats small, often dead, insects. They are brown or black, and slender.

Striped Earwig
This earwig is a brown-red colour and you might spot one with dark stripes. They are most commonly found near water.

Common Cockroach
You might spot this one on rubbish tips, or coming out of the bath, as it loves moist conditions.

German Cockroach
Despite its name, the German cockroach actually comes from North Africa. It is a pest in warehouses and bakeries where it nests in rotting rubbish.

Grasshoppers and Crickets – Spot It

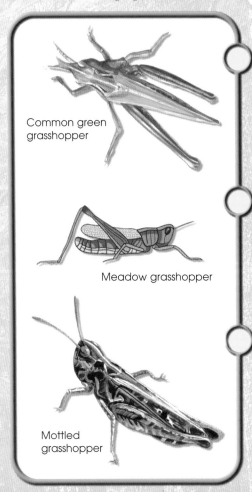

Common green grasshopper

Meadow grasshopper

Mottled grasshopper

Common Green Grasshopper

The common green grasshopper is usually pure green and can be spotted in long grass.

Meadow Grasshopper

The meadow grasshopper is 10–24 mm long. It is usually green, but you might spot one that is a mixture of brown, pink and red.

Mottled Grasshopper

When you hear it sing, you might think that someone is winding up a clock. Their call is a series of soft, fast `zrr` noises that lasts about ten seconds.

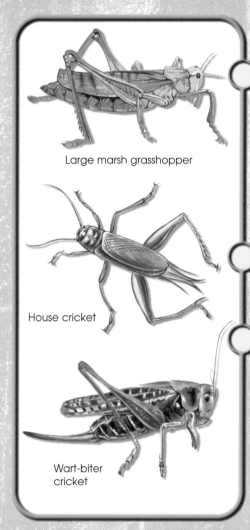

Large marsh grasshopper

House cricket

Wart-biter
cricket

Large Marsh Grasshopper

At 28–32 mm long, the large marsh grasshopper is huge! Its body and wings are clearly marked in lime green, yellow and black. Look for the black and yellow bands on its hind legs.

House Crickets

House crickets are 15 mm long and mainly nocturnal.

Wart-biter Cricket

The wart-biter is so-called because it was once believed that they could cure warts by biting them off human skin. They are now quite rare, so be pleased with yourself if you spot this one!